Just Around
the Corner

Just Around the Corner
Poems About the Seasons

Leland B. Jacobs
pictures by Jeff Kaufman

A Bill Martin Book
Henry Holt and Company • New York

Bill Martin Jr, Ph.D., has devoted his life to the education of young children. *Bill Martin Books* reflect his philosophy: that children's imaginations are opened up through the play of language, the imagery of illustration, and the permanent joy of reading books.

For B. H. J. especially—L. B. J.

For Julie, Anna, and Daniel—J. K.

Henry Holt and Company, Inc. / *Publishers since 1866*
115 West 18th Street, New York, New York 10011

Henry Holt is a registered trademark of Henry Holt and Company, Inc.

Text copyright © 1993 by Allan D. Jacobs
Illustrations copyright © 1993 by Jeff Kaufman
All rights reserved.
Published in Canada by Fitzhenry & Whiteside Ltd., 91 Granton Drive, Richmond Hill, Ontario L4B 2N5.
Originally published in slightly different form in 1964 by Holt, Rinehart and Winston,
with illustrations by John E. Johnson.

A CIP catalog record for this book is available from the Library of Congress.

ISBN 0-8050-2676-2

First Edition—1993

Printed in the United States of America on acid-free paper. ∞

10 9 8 7 6 5 4 3 2 1

Contents

AUT

TASTE OF PURPLE

Grapes hang purple
In their bunches,
Ready for
September lunches.
Gather them, no
Minutes wasting.
Purple is
Delicious tasting.

U M N

QUANDARY

Out in the grasses,
  Cleverly hid,
A voice keeps calling,
  "Katy did!"

"Katy did!"
  The voice will cry.
"Did what?" I ask,
  But there's no reply.

The voice repeats,
  In the weeds and clover,
"Katy did! Katy did!"
  Over and over.

So I'll never learn
  From the voice that's hid
Just what it was
  That Katy did.

GOOD COMPANY

When other flowers
   Have gone away,
The goldenrod
   And asters stay.

The asters with
   Their purple blooms,
The goldenrod
   In yellow plumes,

Linger, though
   The others flee,
And keep
   October company.

AUTUMN LEAVES

Green leaves,
　Yellow leaves,
　　Red leaves, and brown,
　　　Falling,
　　　　Falling,
　　　　　Blanketing the town.
　　　　　Oak leaves,
　　　　　　Maple leaves,
　　　　　　　Apple leaves, and pear,
　　　　　　　Falling,
　　　　　　　　Whispering,
　　　　　　　　　"Autumn's in the air!"
　　　　　　　　　Big leaves,
　　　　　　　　　　Little leaves,
　　　　　　　　　　　Pointed leaves, and round,
　　　　　　　　　　　Falling,
　　　　　　　　　　　　Nestling,
　　　　　　　　　　　　　Carpeting the ground.

AUTUMN BIRD SONG

Over the housetops,
Over the trees,
Winging their way
In a stiff fall breeze,

A flock of birds
Is flying along
Southward, for winter,
Singing a song,

Singing a song
They all like to sing.
"We'll see you again
When it's spring, spring, spring."

ON HALLOWEEN

Kitten, kitten,
  Don't go out.
Witches are flying
  All about.

Kitten, kitten,
  Stay inside
Or you'll be off
  On a broomstick ride.

It's Halloween,
  And witches roam,
So kitten, kitten,
  You must stay home.

FAT OLD WITCH

The strangest sight
I've ever seen
Was a fat old witch
In a flying machine.

The witch flew high,
The witch flew low,
The witch flew fast,
The witch flew slow,
The witch flew up,
The witch flew down,
She circled all
Around the town.
Then, turning left
And turning right,
She disappeared
Into the night.

The fat old witch
In a flying machine
Is the strangest sight
I've ever seen.
Of course it happened
On Halloween.

WHAT WITCHES DO

The witches don their pointed hats,
The witches croak and croon,
The witches ride their broomsticks
Away beyond the moon.

The witches don their flowing cloaks,
The witches stir their brew,
The witches chant their magic spells
All the dark hours through.

The witches stroke their big black cats,
They comb their locks of gray,
Yet when the first faint daylight comes,
The witches hide away.

WIN

SNOW PRINTS

Track of stag
    And track of doe
Print the pages
    Of the snow—
Print the snow
    With message clear,
Saying, stag and doe
    Were here.
But what their errand,
    Where they sped,
In the snow prints
    Can't be read.

14

TER

WHAT DO YOU SAY?

What do you say
    To a bear that's waiting,
Just about ready
    For hibernating?

You don't say "Good evening,"
    It wouldn't seem right,
You'd not say "Good morning,"
    Or even "Good night."

I suppose you could say,
    "Good sleeping! Good rest!"
Or maybe "Good winter!"
    Would be the best.

BEAR COAT

The polar bear, the
    Polar bear—
He has a handsome
    Coat to wear.

But, while it's thick and
    Warm and white,
He has to wear it day and
    Night.

And when the summer
    Comes, poor brute,
He wears it for his swimming
    Suit.

Although his coat is thought
    So fine,
I'm very glad that it's
    Not mine.

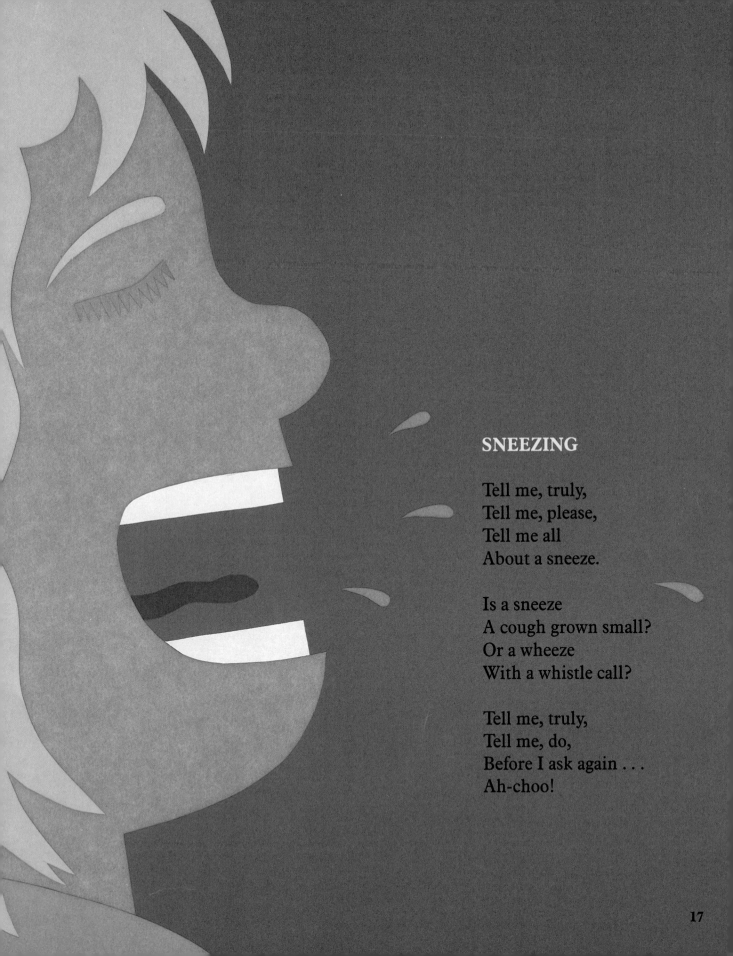

SNEEZING

Tell me, truly,
Tell me, please,
Tell me all
About a sneeze.

Is a sneeze
A cough grown small?
Or a wheeze
With a whistle call?

Tell me, truly,
Tell me, do,
Before I ask again . . .
Ah-choo!

NEW YEAR BELLS

A bell that was big
    And gruff and bold
Bade good-bye
    To the year grown old.

A bell that was small
    And tinkled clear
Called greetings
    To the youngest year.

Then all the bells
    Joined the merry din
And the bright new year
    Was welcomed in.

18

RAIN SONG

Spring rain is pink rain,
    For petals sweet and fair,
Summer rain is rainbow rain,
    With colors everywhere.

The rain of fall is brown rain,
    With leaves that whirl and blow,
And the winter rain is white rain,
    But we call it snow.

SPR

KITE

Tug the string, kite,
   Pull it, please;
Sail above
   The tallest trees.

Climb to where
   The white clouds run;
Stretch and scamper
   Toward the sun.

Float and fly, kite,
   Tug the string;
Show the world
   You're glad it's spring.

20

ING

SOLUTION

When I went out to play
 The day had just begun.
"Put on your coat," said the wind.
 "Take off your coat," said the sun.

Now who was in the right?
 And which advice was better?
I solved the problem for myself—
 I just put on my sweater.

FOR ST. PATRICK'S DAY

Fiddle tune,
Fiddle play,
Fiddle for St. Patrick's Day.
Tell of shamrock,
Fair to see,
Tell of Blarney's
Mystery.
Tell about
The fairy ring.
Fiddle sing,
Fiddle play,
Fiddle for St. Patrick's Day.

IT'S SPRING!

Snapdragon, snap,
Toadstool, turn,
Pussy willow, purr,
Fireweed, burn,
Black-eyed Susan, wink,
Sweet William, sing,
Forget-me-not, remember
It's Spring! Spring! Spring!

Catnip, nip,
Dandelion, roar,
Dogwood, bark,
Pitcher plant, pour,
Bee balm, buzz,
Bluebell, ring,
Jack-in-the-pulpit
Preach today,
It's Spring! Spring! Spring!

OUT IN THE RAIN

Willie Duck and Wallie Duck
Went out in the rain to play,
Splashing in the puddles
In a very careless way.

Neither had a raincoat
And neither had a hat,
But their mother didn't worry
Or fret about that.

Willie Duck and Wallie Duck
For almost an hour,
Without any rubbers on
Played in a shower.

Of course their mother saw them,
But she didn't scold.
She didn't even tell them
That they'd both catch cold.

Willie Duck and Wallie Duck
Were wet clear through.
And what about their mother?
She was out there too!

LAST WORD

Today the April rain
Is flecked with snow:
Soft little flakes, wind-tossed,
Run in the rain—lost—
Trying to explain
That winter should remain,
Letting us know
That winter hates to go.

SUM

SHADOWS

The shadows of bushes
   Are much too small;
They hardly cover
   A child at all.

But the shadows of trees
   Are long and wide,
So that's the place
   Where I like to hide.

If I hide in the bushes,
   Everyone sees
My arms and hands
   Or my legs and knees.

But deep in the shadow
   Of a tree,
Not even the sun
   Can discover me.

MER

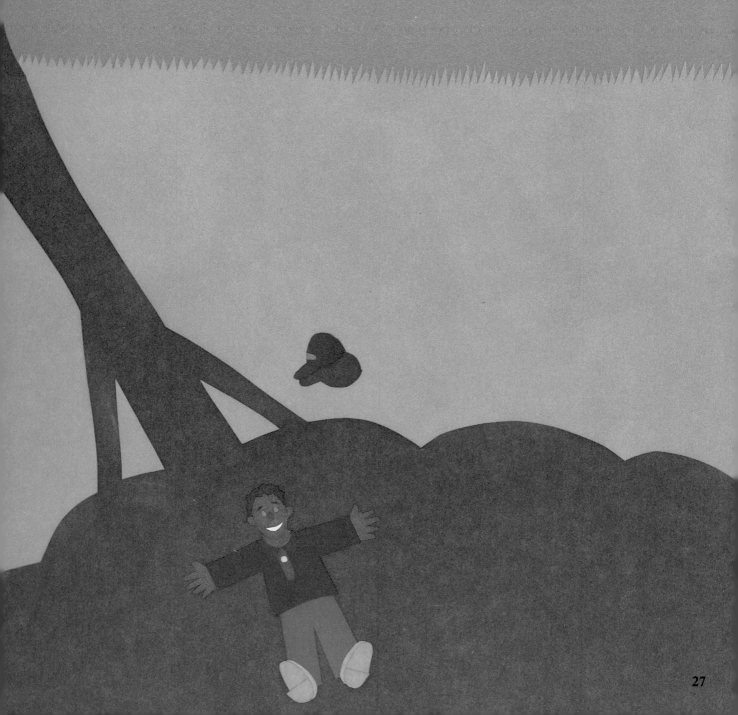

THE SUN

Although it is gold,
    It isn't a locket;
Though shaped like a coin,
    It fits no pocket.

It hasn't a ladder,
    But it can climb.
It's much like a clock
    For telling the time.

It gives itself, free,
    To child and man,
But nobody touches it.
    Nobody can.

SHORE

A shore is the place
   To play in the sand.
A shore is the place
   For digging a well.
A shore is the place
   To watch for a ship.
A shore is the place
   For finding a shell.
A shore is the place
   To lie in the sun
And watch the waves
   As they roll and run.
A shore is the place
   Where gulls fly free—
A shore is a wonderful
   Place to be.

NIGHT SONG

When the sun has set
And night has come,
The insect chorus
Starts to hum.

And nothing else
Is there to hear,
But the insect voices
Soft and clear.

The insects hum
In sweet delight,
Singing their praises
Of the night.

WOODPECKER

On the telephone pole
       I rap, rap, rap.
On the trunk of a tree
       I tap, tap, tap.
I peck, peck, peck,
       And I knock, knock, knock.
But don't turn the key
       And open the lock.
I never stop at a door to call,
For I'm not the visiting kind at all.
And if you should ask me in to play,
I'd simply have to fly away.